To My Beautiful Friend Margaret,

You inspire me and encourage my heart with your loving kindness. May these poems speak to your heart.

Love you,
Betty

P.S. May you some day write your own poetry.

In the Hidden Corners of *My Heart*

By

Kathryn Sojka-Fairchild

WESTBOW
PRESS®
A DIVISION OF THOMAS NELSON
& ZONDERVAN

Copyright © 2015 Kathryn Sojka-Fairchild.

Design and Layout, Paola Vera

All rights reserved. No part of this book may be used or reproduced by any means, graphic, electronic, or mechanical, including photocopying, recording, taping or by any information storage retrieval system without the written permission of the author except in the case of brief quotations embodied in critical articles and reviews.

WestBow Press books may be ordered through booksellers or by contacting:

WestBow Press
A Division of Thomas Nelson & Zondervan
1663 Liberty Drive
Bloomington, IN 47403
www.westbowpress.com
1 (866) 928-1240

Because of the dynamic nature of the Internet, any web addresses or links contained in this book may have changed since publication and may no longer be valid. The views expressed in this work are solely those of the author and do not necessarily reflect the views of the publisher, and the publisher hereby disclaims any responsibility for them.

Any people depicted in stock imagery provided by Thinkstock are models, and such images are being used for illustrative purposes only. Certain stock imagery © Thinkstock.

ISBN: 978-1-4908-6039-8 (sc)
ISBN: 978-1-4908-6040-4 (hc)
ISBN: 978-1-4908-6041-1 (e)

Library of Congress Control Number: 2014920523

Print information available on the last page.

WestBow Press rev. date: 9/9/2015

Dedication

This book is dedicated to all children everywhere who are threatened with inadequate food, hunger, sickness and those enslaved by human trafficking. May the proceeds of this book help improve their health, and overall well-being.

Proceeds of this book go to:
"Forever Found"
1464 Madera Road #158
Simi Valley, California 93065

Acknowledgments

Thank you to my mentor and benefactor in this project who wishes to be Anonymous and who encouraged and challenged me to disseminate my poems in this format.

Thank you and love to my sons, Mark, David and Steven Sojka and their beautiful families who help me just by loving me and being supportive of my writing. You are my life and my heart.

Thanks to the ministry "Forever Found" who joined hands with me and allowed me to walk beside them on their chosen path.

Finally, and most importantly, thanks to our Almighty God for the absolute gift and privilege of this opportunity of being able to help my brothers and sisters in pain, trials and tribulations to find shelter in the arms of our Merciful and Loving God.

Introduction

Kathryn Sojka-Fairchild began writing poetry at age 7. Then she switched to prose and was convinced she would write a novel "someday". Then, as her children became teenagers and great tragedy struck her life she once again turned to poetry. Ten years later as great life changes once again turned her life upside down, she returned to poetry with renewed interest.

Of this latest stage in her writing Kathryn says "something changed. As I wrote most of my poems, it was mystifying — the poems just appeared in my mind, fully composed and I would write as fast as I could so I wouldn't 'lose' the poem". Some she had to work on a bit and there were quite a few that had no ties to spirituality, but the ones that concerned the spiritual seemed to be just "given" to her. Friends began to wonder if these were gifts of the Holy Spirit because the poems were spiritual. She once looked in the Bible in Galatians 5:22 where the gifts of the Holy Spirit are enumerated and she discovered that Poetry is not listed as a gift. "I am sure it was just an oversight" she says with a twinkle in her eyes. Her great degree of Empathy enabled her to write about things not in her actual experience, especially those in the chapter, "Out Of the Book".

She had often wished she could use her poems to help children. In 2012 she completely lost any interest or motivation in continuing her writing. She remembers sitting in her den and suddenly asked God "Do you have any plans for these poems for I have lost any desire to even look at them anymore." Suddenly she had a mentor, a professional typist who knew how to lay out the copy in book form, an editor and a publisher. Shortly thereafter, she connected with an organization whose ministry addressed exactly what she wanted to do with her poems. She could sell her books and support the ministry to which they were both drawn. "I have read that coincidence is just another name for God."

However these poems came about, they certainly have been a gift and privilege for Kathryn. She prays they "will help children who, through no fault of their own, find themselves in devastating circumstances".

KATHRYN lives in Southern California. She's been widowed twice, is the mother of three sons and three stepsons, daughters-in-law that she loves and admires and says she is "blessed by the most beautiful grandchildren in the world!"

She says, "Life has presented me with many challenges, but God's presence has always been there. It seems the hard times tend to teach the most lessons. There were times that as soon as one lesson was learned, another was put in my path. But God is faithful and He promised He would be with us always."

Finally, to my readers she says, "Please pay no attention to your wallet and bank book, but take the time to look and see how rich we children of God really are."

Chapters

On My Journey (Learning) • 13

About "Him" • 45

A Merry Heart Is Good Medicine • 61

Petition • 73

Out of the Book • 81

Easter • 91

Christmas • 99

Hope • 105

Seeking The Ruin of Souls • 109

Questions • 115

Second Thoughts For When You Have a Minute • 131

On My Journey
(Learning)

The Pottery of the Lord

Bits of bitterness, as mosaic pieces, being brought together to make a whole.
A broken bit of suffering
fit together with a piece of brokenness with a sliver of anger brought together to create a corner of forgiveness.
Handles made of open arms
replacing pointing fingers.
Humility grouts judgement together with a recognition of our own selfishness and disobedience.
Cracks of reluctance to confess, repent, redeem
(when our own life has broken) show stress marks in the work.
Mercy, mercy we cry to the Master Artist.
Be the glue that pulls this creation of faith together.
He never gives up on us.
He understands brokenness and can make us whole;
Into a masterpiece.
My soul is crippled but my body is seen as whole.
How many crippled and handicapped enter our lives unacknowledged because we cannot see their brokenness?
Treat kindly those who cross your path
for you might be the straw that broke the fragile spirit or
you could be the glue that helps anchor
a broken soul together.

Song of Privilege

"Blessed Be The Name Of the Lord".
Is a song that I
lift up to You
from the music of my soul.

Your Precious Name:
So Holy,
trampled,
Beloved,
misused,
Life giving,
profaned.

Your name is beyond Wonder
on my lips.
I will hold up Your Name
in reverence.

I will whisper in my heart,
"Blessed Be The Name of the Lord"
every time I hear someone
using Your Name in vain.

I offer this small gesture
as reparation, as a "forgive us",
as an "I'm sorry"
for the wounds to Your Sacred Heart.

Exodus 20:7

Disciples Prayer

My candle
is so small
and
the darkness is
so big.

By myself
I can do nothing.
Let your love
shine through me.

Your hands
were nailed to the Cross.
Use my hands to minister to others.

Your feet
were impaled on that tree.
Use my feet to go to those in need.

Your side
was wounded.
Use my words, my pain
to bring compassion to others.

They lay your body
in a tomb.
Use me to love others
into the Body of Christ,
your Church.

A Life of Song

Singing His song
silently with our deeds.

Oh, what we say
without words.

Others watch, not realizing
they are seeing what we say
about our Faith.

Our quiet joy thunders
a message subliminally.

Our soul has no voice.

It's our loving kindness
that speaks to the world.

A message of living
that speaks only through Grace.

Our deeds tell others
when spoken words would
fall empty, unheard.

We sing a song of Christian witness
with our lives.

Walk the Walk

Go out into the world.
Show your faith to those
who cannot or will not
listen to your testimony.
As Mother Teresa
proselytized and evangelized
by her touch, gentle words
and the look of love in her eyes.
Service to others is our witness.
It is our consequence to
love God, love our neighbors.
To be of service.
We are authorized to act like Jesus:
with no judgement,
with love, without condemnation
at work, at home,
in the community.
Reaching to all with love.
This all requires hope, mercy,
joy and much prayer.
For we are a people chosen
and set apart.
Thank you, God.

ECUMENICAL BROTHERHOOD

Each of our lives sing
a different song.
Come sing
in harmony with me.
If you so choose,
fall into step beside me
and we will sing
the same song.
I'll not insist
you walk on my path
and sing my melody
for I do not know
what path you see,
what music you hear.
So too, do not push me
from the path laid before me.
Do not insist
I sing your offertory
for our purpose and destination
are the same.
I am called to sing my song,
and you to sing yours.
I may hear
the choir of the Clouds.
You may hear the chorus of the Trees.
Not better or best,
just different.

(Cont'd next page)

(Cont'd *Ecumenical Brotherhood*)

Blessed are we
if we can walk
side by side
and harmonize.
I respect your path, your journey.
I try to hear your music
if it's different from mine.
Will we not be enriched
as we hear each other's song?
Our destination is the same
and at the end of our journey
I pray
we will arrive home
singing praises to our God
together.

Psalm 133:1

Diversity

Different gifts
are given at
different times
to
different people.

Isn't it wonderful
that we all are a
bit different?

Wouldn't it be boring
if we were all alike?

Look for and treasure
the gifts
you see in others.

It widens your world,
broadens your appreciation,
stretches your mind
to possibilities.

Always ask God
for a grateful heart.

It will change your life.

ACHILLES HEEL OF MANKIND

For salvation of our soul,
we've devised a clever "bit."
We simply handle the matter
by just ignoring it!

For if we do not "see" it
we have no obligation
to face that aspect of our lives:
an unwelcome revelation.

For that would mean we're grown up.
Our choices decide our fate.
Most grow old; we don't grow up -
(An acknowledgement we hate!)

2 /Corinthians 4:3-6

Spiritual Desert

My voice seems gone,
My heart lies as dormant,
yet there is this great
burning, yearning to burst into flames.
To burn high and free
to thank you, to love you, to express
Soul to Spirit
this love I have for you.

My voice is in a prison.
I'm unable to express what burns,
yearns in my heart.
Held behind a barrier of inability
to relate, to express
Finite to Infinity.
My love, my gratitude, my wonder
are inadequate
as is the voice of my heart.

I can only stand,
with humility,
and merely say
I love you Lord.

It seems not enough.

Romans 8:26-27

Ferme la Bouche!*

When you criticize them,
you criticize me.

For we are all part of one another.

When you judge them,
you judge me.

For we are all connected.

When you hate them,
you hate me.

For we are all part of one.

*French for "close the mouth"

Contemplation

ALONE is peace, quiet solitude.
LONELY is anxiety.

ALONE is sorting through your own thoughts, realizing your priorities.
LONELY is thinking of your own pain.

ALONE is growing, finding your own worth, your joy.
LONELY is feeling temporary.

ALONE is finding the dignity of self.
LONELY is needing others to make yourself real.

ALONE is realizing you're responsible for your own happiness.
LONELY is expecting someone else to make you happy.

ALONE is gazing at pools of quiet reflections in your mind.
LONELY is sloshing through puddles of self pity.

ALONE is taking the time to look at the maturity
of your emotions and soul.
LONELY is looking inside yourself and finding no one's there!

I Am Learning

I am learning …

Rather than running to God
And pounding on His chest,
And breathlessly, fearfully
Pouring out my fears, angers,
Handing Him my list of "fix-its"

to instead …

Reach out and
Silently and quietly
Into my heart,
Feel the calmness,
The serenity
That He brings to my inner being.

Philippians 4:6-7

The Romance of the Night

A beautiful night
Peaceful, quiet,
the slightest breeze
fluttering around me.

The flowers I lavish
with such care
in my days now thank me
with their slight perfume.

I am here now,
where I'm meant to be
though unknowing of
Your plans for me.

Our lives and minds
are finite
and You are infinite.
Who can fully know You?

I silently acknowledge You
lifting my thoughts and heart
where prayers and heaven
meet and kiss.

Why Would You Want to Live That Way?

HATE
A strange poison that afflicts the hater, not the hated.

RESENTMENT
Acid eating away your entire personality.
Unseen disfigurement as you twist and scar unseen.

BITTERNESS
A withering of soul.
A turning inward like a dying leaf.
Scoliosis of the soul.

LOVE
is the healer.
God is Love. Seek Him out.

Hurry!

Go to the Owner's Manual.
Go to the Fix-it Book.
Go to the Book of Instruction,
When for answers you look.

Go to the Inspired Word.
Go quickly, don't be idle.
Find Wisdom that's been saved for you.
Go and read your Bible.

2 Timothy 3:16-17

Spirit Seeking

In the quiet of worship
our praise rises like flame to you.

Burning with love and yearning.

Spirit seeking Holy Spirit.

We proclaim your death
in Thanksgiving for Eternal Life.

Opression

She wears a shroud
of anxiety and strife.
Worry has become
her Master's thesis on life.

Day and night
she wears that shroud.
Because faith whispers
and fears are loud.

SALVATION FOUND

He climbed over the detritus of his life.
Seeing nothing, left or right.
Keeping his eyes on the prize
as he bypasses distractions and temptations.
The Destroyer brings
invasive thoughts to his mind.
He ignores this and re-fixes his eyes
on the prize up on the mountain top.
A life transformed.
He found "the Way the Truth and the Light".
On and on he goes with Joy and Fulfillment,
having found the meaning of his life.

Look and See

Bless those ahead of us
for they can show us
we still have further to go.

Bless those who are behind us
for they show us
how far we have come
and what God has done for us.

1st verse —— Philippians 3:17, 4:9
2nd verse —— Philippians 3:12-14

Law of Physics

"FOR EVERY ACTION THERE IS
AN EQUAL AND OPPOSITE REACTION."

… so, if there is goodness, we must
accept that evil exists.

"ENERGY CANNOT BE CREATED NOR DESTROYED,
IT CAN ONLY CHANGE FORM."

… to me, this argues the existence of the Soul.

I Am "I Am", You Are "To Be"

There's a deep, dark hole
in the center of my Soul
and I look for ways
to fill it up.

Wandering here and there
with concern, despairing care
looking for the cure
for my emptiness.

Bitter thoughts emerge,
twisted rage, a selfish urge.
Am I the only one
to search for more?

Sampling that and this —
is this all; what is a-miss?
Others all around seem
satisfied with what's at hand.

Searching both day and night
for the answer, for the Light
to open up, to dawn upon
my unfulfilled heart.

Out of that inner place
outstretched arms reach to embrace
a "Something" hovering 'round
the edges of my night.

(Cont'd next page)

(Cont'd *I AM "I AM", YOU ARE "TO BE"*)

A nameless voice calls to me:
"I have come to set you free
from this aching search
to fulfill the inner me."

"Become known to me.
I am "I AM", you are "To Be"
who you've achingly known
you could be all along."

A Saviour comes to call.
He is enough. He is all.
The dawning comes as
puzzle pieces of my life now fit.

HE is the Light I've sought.
My life is NOT for naught.
I've truly been so blind
I cannot see.

A treasure so true and rare,
I've had to search for where
You've been, and I found you
deep within my own heart.

(In this poem I tried to imagine how people manage without God.
I can't remember when I didn't know Him.)

Did You Hear a Page Turn?

Did you hear a page turn
when that broken wing and
shattered cup were the
portrait of your Life?

Did you see a road sign
when you were suddenly
left alone and you seemed
to have no direction?

Did you finally see a choice
through your tears
or had grief
become your identity?

Did you face your fears
and find that
you were Bigger
than the Problem?

Did silence feel empty,
then your soul opened
and you realized instead
it was a place to grow?

Did the music stop
and you found that
you were now the conductor
of your own symphony?

(Cont'd next page)

(Cont'd *Did You Hear a Page Turn?*)

Life goes on even if you opt out.

There's all the color, warmth and
joy of breathing through each day
or
have you been holding your breath?

SONG OF THE NIGHT

The sounds of the night
croon seemingly only to me.
The unheard symphony of moon and stars.
Darkness humming heartily of
serenity or fear depending on who
you choose to be your conductor.
A soundless orchestra of
individual prayers
melding to a crescendo
in the Universe.

Elucidate and Meditate

Do we really
think and pay attention
to the Lord's prayer?
When we ask …
"Forgive us our trespasses
as we forgive those who
trespass against us?"

Do we contemplate and meditate on
how forgiving others will determine
how we will be forgiven?

We've said and read the prayer
so often that we say it by rote
and don't really think about
the words we are saying.

Take time to say it slowly
and meditate on those words.

It will change your life.

Dark Night of the Soul

God given to teach us
how empty and wretched
we are without him.
A withdrawing of
a sense of His Presence.
Desolate.
Empty.
To know You,
to hear Your voice,
to feel Your presence,
then all withdrawn.
A final lesson
for the Saints
to journey on,
to persevere,
when we no longer
feel the truth of the Scriptures,
"Lord, I am with You always".
But we go on
in our faith;
lonely travelers in our Faith
we finish our journey,
knowing we cannot turn
from Your Love.

We still seek You.

My Lord and My God

King of Kings and Lord of Lords
who is worshiped by Angels.
By the Universe and all therein.
Whose Name is above all names.
Who sits at the right hand of the Father.
How is it that when you manifested on earth,
you were born in a cave with a dirt floor,
rather than in a palace fit for the Prince of Peace?
A place humbling to everyone by its' aura.
Amidst animals whose soft calling welcomed you
rather than a celestial choir.
A manger for a cradle, filled with hay, food for animals;
reminding us, in a way,
that Jesus is the Bread of Life.
For our Souls and for Everlasting Life.
Humble Shepherds came to you to see your glory
foreshadowing how we are drawn to you,
seeing your Glory by your Grace.
Wise men came to you
perhaps to teach that wisdom is always in your presence;
that coming to you is the ultimate wisdom for Man.
Was this all meant as a parable to show us
that we must be humble before God can use us?
The lesson enabled and shown so clearly
by the total obedience of Mary, Joseph and Jesus.

Your death — so violent, vicious, bloody and cruel!
Your death couldn't be gentle.
We had to be shown just how serious and destructive sin is.

(Cont'd next page)

(Cont'd *My Lord and My God*)

That this is what Jesus had to overcome to save us
from Sin and its' resulting Death.
That Sin is so towering and brutally eats at the purity of a Soul.
That each drop of blood, each moment of overwhelming suffering
built a barricade for us, to shield us as we enter into the Kingdom.
Your Love is so overpowering and awesome
I can only humbly bow my head in its' presence.
Speechless.
With nothing to offer you but my love and obedience.

About "Him"

QUIETLY

God speaks
through the
common,
ordinary,
occurrences
of daily life.

Not always the earthquake,
thunder,
the parting of a sea.

Our Soul calls us to
simple thoughts,
simple lives,
time set apart
to hear
His voice,
to feel
His presence.

Listen to the sounds of
Silence.

Profound words
are not needed
as much as
Profound Listening.

1 Kings 19:11-12

Soon, Lord?

One day, after the night
all will be new,
all will be understood.

One day, the unseen answers
to our prayers
will stand before us.

One day we shall tremble
as we hear Him say,
"As you forgave,
I will now forgive you."

One day our ears will hear,
as nature testifies,
that Jesus Christ is Lord.

One day we shall see the face of God as
the curtain is drawn open,
and Light floods the Darkness.

Lord

You fill up
the empty places
in my heart;
places where love
has been and gone.

You fill up
the empty places
in my life;
with meaning so rich and fulfilling.

Those whose spiritual lives
die unborn
are in a great emptiness and poverty
of which they are unaware.

How Great Thou Art, O God

You fill my heart with gladness.
How great Thou art.

You bring to mind acts of kindness I can do.
How great Thou art.

You made my path clear to me.
How great Thou art.

You gently give me correction
when I still my mind to hear you.
How great Thou art.

You have blessed me with a wonderful family
and filled my heart with love for them.
How great Thou art.

Your light has carried me through the darkness
when it threatened to overwhelm me.
How great Thou art.

See Him in a Flower

Creations of nature showing us your face.
For we have been told we cannot
see Your face and live.
You are so holy.

Do you show us who You are
through nature, Your creations?

The Grand Canyon reminded me
that You are bigger than my mind can comprehend.
That in bringing Your nature into my understanding
I make You too small.

The Sun, for me,
reflects the Light of your Goodness.
Your Holiness being the Light of the World.
For Your Light is so much more.

The energy and force of
earthquakes and volcanoes
give me a glimpse of Your power.
You, who can do anything.

You are
Creator of the Universe,
of man
in all his complexities.

I struggle for understanding.
Achieving tiny steps forward
as my journey,
so exciting, so profound, continues.

You Are ...

You are the dawn
and the gentle twilight.

You are the day
and the quiet of night.

You are the Spring
and also the Fall.

You are the One
who died for us all.

Who am I to be given this gift?

You fill up all the empty places
in my Soul and in my Life.
You elevate my
Gladness into Joy.

For You are the fulfillment
for the empty spaces
in my heart
and in my life.

My cup does indeed floweth over.

Come Near

"I love you"
He calls to me.
"Be the best
that you can be."

"Come rise to the fulness
of all that is you;
reborn in Me
who makes all things new."

"O, my beloved
hear thou My call.
You belong to my Son.
You're the richest of all."

"Come, rest in my arms
for in you I delight.
For my yoke is easy
and my burden is light."

Joy!

Oh, my Lord God,
just to know you exist
has my heart breathless
with giddiness,
my Soul dancing in delight.

The wonder and thanksgiving
has my Spirit twirling in joy.
And I thank you, thank you, thank you
that I know you are "there".

Your Word tells me
that You called me.
Then You gave me the Grace
to hear Your call!

I know that I am loved
even beyond my understanding
and I am filled and uplifted.
How lovely.

The Sacrifice, the Covenant

And I cried, with defiance,
into the wind …

"LOVE CONQUERS ALL"

Then I remembered
with humility,
that, yes, Love* had conquered all!

1 John 4:8

*"God is Love"

Love Letter to Jesus

You are my Soul's definition
without words.

You are the horizon;
I sense no beginning and no end.

You are the clouds,
beautiful and ever-changing.

You are the mountains,
drawing my eyes and thoughts ever upward.

I Am

Stands as an
irrefutable witness
and fairly shouts a testimony
of His presence.

The work of His hand
from infinitesimal to infinite
silently waiting for us to notice
their existence as proof of I AM.

The unending horizon
a silent allegory:
"As it was in the beginning,
is now and ever shall be."

The Alpha and Omega concept of Him
too large to grasp.
Our finite minds groping
for the reality of infinity.

I Hear You Lord

Come out of the Darkness.
Come into the Light.
I call to your Soul.
For in you I delight.

As a moth is drawn
to the flickering flame,
draw near to Me.
Honor my name.

Listen to me!
I'll refresh you anew.
Be all you can be.
Do all you can do.

Allow me to come
to your broken heart.
I'll give your life meaning.
We're not meant to part.

Joyful, Joyful

Let the mountains sing acapella.
To the accompaniment of trees clapping.
The sea roars bass.
The flowers, a sweet soprano.
Rocks keep a subtle beat.

Shout with Joy all the earth!
For the Lord is on His throne
and praise fills the universe.
Glory, glory sing the Angels.
Let the air be filled with the majesty of His love.

Nature's exploding with the Joy of His existence.
The very air breathes His names of
Righteousness, Justice and Love.
We kneel at His footstool, and bow our heads,
overcome with Thanksgiving.

A Merry Heart Is Good Medicine

Proverbs 17:22

ATTITUDE BEATITUDE

BLESS THOSE WHO TRY TO FIND YOU
IN THE CLAMOR OF THEIR DAYS.
Bless those who try to lose you,
understanding not your ways.
BLESS THOSE WHO TREAT THEIR BROTHERS
WITH RESPECT AMIDST ALL STRIFE.
Bless those who think Commercials
teach the meaning of all life.
BLESS THOSE WHO FEED THE HUNGRY,
SOILING HANDS TO DO YOUR WILL.
Bless those who murmur pieties,
ignoring needs they could fulfill.
BLESS THOSE WHO PRAY FOR OTHERS,
FROM GOOD WORKS THEY NEVER REST.
Bless those who are so very sure,
they always know what's best.
BLESS THOSE WHO PRAISE AND WORSHIP YOU
AS AUTHOR OF CREATION.
Bless those who veil their words and kill
their neighbors reputation.
BLESS THOSE WHO WORSHIP PIOUSLY.
YOUR GREATNESS THEY REALIZE.
Bless those who manipulate
and constantly criticize.
BLESS THOSE WHO WORK TO IMPROVE THEIR SOULS
WITH NO IFS, OR ANDS, OR BUTS.
Bless those who meddle in my life.
Dear lord, they drive me nuts!

Luke 6:27

Think About It!

It has been suggested
that Jesus was more likely
a stone mason
because there are so few trees
in the Holy Land.

But ...

I really like the idea
that He was a carpenter.
I know the He's had
to "hammer" me into
shape now and then.

(You too?)

Pay Attention!

As I go my busy way,
through my trite and shallow day.
A world around me I can't see
as Angels 'round watch over me.

Coincidence? I pause and fuss
as God remains anonymous.
I, so busy, plot and plan
thinking all controlled by man.

The tides, the universe, I forgot.
I measure what control I've got.
I think it all depends on me.
As unseen worlds I do not see.

A master plan, you ask of me?
I don't believe what I can't see.
If His word I'd stop and read,
I'd see He answers every need.

My dear Jesus, need I mention,
knocks on my heart to get attention.
I really do — I think instead,
He should be knocking on my head!

CAN YOU MOVE?

Welcome to our church!
We're so glad to see you!
(Just don't ask me to move
from the end of the pew!)
Our pastor is wonderful.
Our parishioners are "divine."
(I will not move over!
that end seat is mine.)
As a perish we're loving,
we're roses in clover.
(The end's my divine right
and I will NOT move over.)
We don't realize how silly we look,
stubbornly sitting, clutching hymnbook,
making you walk sideways or up on the riser,
'cuz I'm not gonna move, I'm a seat miser!
Now those with a walker,
a limp or a cane
deserve that end spot
and need not to explain.
There may be a soul
who needs that end seat
so crawl right on over
but watch for their feet!
There may be a reason
they sit on the end.
Their back may be hurting,
their knees may not bend.
But, how as a Christian
do we otherwise excuse
our ungracious, unloving
resistance to move?
Wouldn't it be nice, wouldn't it be kind
if you just got up and moved your behind?

IM HOW OLD?

(My 7oth Birthday)

Why did no one tell me
what shape I would be in?
Hair on my head is thinning,
but growing under my chin!

Why did no one tell me
what a foe gravity would be?
That parts I've always been proud of
would end up by my knee?

    Tweezers and razors
    and depilatory
    are only part of
    my very sad story.

    Knees that crack,
    a back that does groan
    are only part of
    what I bemoan.

    Can't think of names?
    Get out of my way ---
    I'm looking
    for car keys,
    how can they stray?

    Remember a name?
    It takes such a long time.
    With cataracts and glaucoma
    I can't read that sign!

    My waist, my neck,
    where did they go?
    I think and walk
    so very, very slow.

(Cont'd *All?*)

> I pray, dear Lord
> as my old skin does itch
> that I won't end up
> a crabby old witch!

In a secret place in my heart, I tuck the idea that this is all part of God's plan to help loosen the ties that keep us on earth. Bit by bit we slowly have things taken from us so it's easier for us to let go and enter into the kingdom.

How Can

A sea be tossed.
A soul be lost

Laughter ripple
A drinker tipple

A tongue be part of a shoe
Me be me, Yet you are you

… (and together we are us?)

How I Think I Would Feel If I Were God

I only ask ten things of you.
Only ten laws by which to live.
Is that too much to ask?
You petition me day and night
unto the point of whining.
Do thanks accompany your petitions?
Does praise enter into your lives?
Think of all the problems
you keep out of your lives by keeping My law.
Is common sense beyond you?
You break my commandments
and when troubles multiply you cry
WHY? WHY?

(Be thankful therefore,
that the great "I AM" is your God
and not me!)

PETITION

Reaching

Lord, give me
eyes that see
their purpose here.

Ears that hear
Your call.

Lips that speak
of praise in prayer.

A heart that first
fills with love for You,
overflowing
and then reaches
to all your children.

All Is Grace

I pray for
bigger words than
"Thank You"
to express gratitude
for what You've given to me.

It's as if words
all crowd and crush together
in my throat because
I can't find the exact words
I need to appreciate You.

I pray that
I recognize Grace
when it's in front of me,
until I grow and learn enough
to realize that
All is Grace.

(Grace is unmerited favor from God.)

Steps on My Journey

Expand my Soul, O Lord
so that I may be able to
know more of you,
may love you more sincerely,
have a greater understanding of You
and
feel you in my heart.

I want to see you in the face of others.

I love you, Jesus.

Help me to love you more.

What? What!

This is my Forever
and it's just drifting by.

Hunting for my purpose,
looking for my path.

I walk along the edges
as the sea upon the shore.

Where do I belong?

What is it I'm suppose to do?

I know I was born for a purpose,
but don't understand what it is.

What are my gifts?

I want to know so I can give them
back to You as an offering.

Please

Lord, give me
eyes that see
their purpose here.

Ears that hear
Your call.

Lips that speak
of praise in prayer.

A heart that first
fills with Love for You

overflowing

and then reaches out
to all Your children.

Lead Me, Search Me

Enlarge my Soul, O Lord
so that I might
hold more of you.

Engrave upon the edges
of my heart,
"May my Life be pleasing to you

Amen

later, I found:

Psalm 139:23, 24
(Now a favorite verse)

"Search me, O God,
and know my heart;
test me and know my anxious thoughts.
See if there is any offensive way in me,
and lead me in the way everlasting."

Out of the Book

BLESSED MOTHER

The Heavens stilled and waited
as the Angel came to Earth
to proclaim God's plan for Mary
regarding Jesus' birth.

"I am but a messenger"
he exclaimed to her with care.
Imagine her amazement
to see an Angel standing there!

The Light! It filled her room.
And strange! ... it filled her heart.
There was no fear, only peace
as he explained her part.

"You are truly Blessed
to hear the Fathers call.
So full of Grace, you have your part
to redeem man from the Fall."

"God, the Father, needs a vessel
to bring forth the Divine:
Majestic Love, Redemption,
The Savior of Mankind."

"Who am I to be so honored?
I'm of Joachim and Anne.
How can this be accomplished
for I have known no man"

(Cont'd next page)

(Cont'd *BLESSED MOTHER*)

"How and why — it does confuse me.
Yet, there's nothing more to say;
Only that I'm God's handmaiden
and I love Him. I'll obey."

The Father gave approval.
The Spirit gave a nod.
By obedience and willing heart
she became the Mother of God.

Joseph of Arimathea

(nothing but questions …)

Did you direct the lowering
of His precious body from the cross?
Did you weep and comfort Mary
as she grieved this awesome loss?
Did your arms help, with others,
as He was carried to your tomb?
Did your heart race, your hands shake
as you placed Him in that room?
Was your mind in despair, your thoughts reel
at the madness of what man had done?
Did you understand, at that moment,
you were tending to God's only Son?
Did you wash the spit from that ravaged face
and pull out thorns from His brow?
Did you wash blood from that battered body
and wonder — what is to happen now?
Did you sleep that night, did you understand
what really had happened that day?
Did grief overcome, did you fall to your knees
and cry, Father help me to pray?
Did you know what you did, who you cared for,
who you touched with such loving care?
Did you understand your great privilege?
What a wonder just to be there!

Cana

The scene is at a wedding
The day is nearly done.
The wine was running out.
Mary beckoned to her Son.

"The host is so embarrassed.
From You I need a sign."
"Woman," He gently told her.
"It is not my time."

But, My obedience is to God," He said....
"There can never be another.
His Commandments tell me that I must
honor the word of My Mother."

"So, fill the jugs with water.."
And Lo! It turned to wine!
It was served, people marvelled.
The taste was quite sublime,

Wasn't this just perfect?
This miracle was His first.
He is "Living Water,"
and the miracle quenched their thirst!

No Jury

Abraham, the patriarch,
was the first defense lawyer
in recorded history.

He argued the case
for the condemned cities
of Sodom and Gomorrah.

Abraham lost.

The prosecutor was God.

(Of course, Abraham lost!)

Mary Magdalene

Who are you, Mary Magdalene,
who stood at the foot of the Cross
with Mary, the Mother?
Who, on that Sunday morning
walked to the tomb
and found the Christ gone.
An Angel there to tell you
He is risen.

I sense your bewilderment
and confusion.

What was your destiny,
your purpose
to be privileged to be
at those places
at those specific times?

To see Him in the garden
after the resurrection.
To feel the ecstasy,
to be able to fall on your knees
and cry, "Rabbi!"

Do I envy your place in His life?

I question my courage.

Passover

Passover, Pass-Over
O Angel of Death
with your cold and killing
merciless breath.

Look not upon my baby boy;
Our first,
his Mother's heart.
He's filled life with joy.

See the blood of the Lamb
on our door.
Sacrifice was made.
Leave and return no more.

Death flows through
as a bloody stream.
(Lamentations from the Palace.)
What can they mean?

O God of Israel,
keep us near.
Watch and protect us
through this night of fear.

O God of Abraham
take my hand.
Lead us soon
to the Promised Land.

As you celebrate the miracle of Passover,
may your home and family be blessed by God.

Easter

The First Holy Friday

Silent, silent was the morn'
they crucified my Lord.
They tied Him fast to wait his fate
with roughly braided cord.

They hammerd nails so big and crude
through precious wrists and feet.
They dared not look up at Him
for fears their eyes would meet.

His Mother came upon that hill
and quietly stood apart.
Prophecy was then fulfilled:
"A sword shall pierce her heart."

They lifted up that tree so tall
and roughly set it down.
His diety was ignored, denied.
They mocked with thorns for crown.

The sign above proclaimed to all
"He is the king of the Jews."
In truth, He is the King of Kings
bringing message of Good News.

(Cont'd next page)

(Cont'd *The First Holy Friday*)

Peter heard the cock crow thrice.
Bitter tears he cried.
His fear had overcome him.
Broken, our Lord he denied.

Where were our Lord's disciples?
Waiting near was only one.
John stood by Mother Mary
grieving for her Son.

The Temple curtain it did tear
inside that worship place.
The earth shook hard (was it with fear?)
The Angels turned their face.

If I did stand upon that hill
on that momentous day,
would I have been part of the crowd
or a disciple - - - dare I say?

And how do now I live my life,
now that the deed is done.
Is there a difference in my life
knowing He's God's Son?

Wondering

Do you still wear that Crown of Thorns
that was pressed upon your head?
Are the marks still on your hands and feet?
Can you see the wounds that bled?

Does your heart still pound in sorrow
as you contemplate the loss
of souls who don't claim victory
and redemption by the Cross?

When you cried out, "It is finished!"
Did the hosts of Angels weep
as you paid the price for heaven,
for the covenant we keep?

Do your tears fall down from heaven
as you see man's starving life;
needing food for soul and spirit,
craving respite from all strife?

Do believers come to Heaven
borne upon an Angel's wing?
Will they shout with joy and triumph,
"You're a child of Christ, the King?"

Do I always see the path
set before me by the Son?
Do I have ears that listen?
Will I hear — "My child, well done"?

2 Peter 1:10-13

Abandoned

Did Heaven hear the hammer fall
as nails pierced His flesh?
Did earth resound with shudders
that came from Mary's breast?

Did Disciples hear the tearing
of gristle and of bone?
Did they understand — soon
He'd be upon His throne?

Did their terror blind them
when He was nailed upon that tree?
Did they hear His cries to God,
"Have You abandoned Me?"*

Where did they go that evening?
Did they scatter, did they hide?
Did they hold each other
as one by one they cried?

Did they comfort Mary?
What would We have done?
Do we hold it in our hearts
He's God's only Son?

*Psalm 22

Good Friday Meditation

Seraphim standing with bowed heads,
Cherubim silent;
Angels in awe.
The earth in wonder.
Birds voices stilled.
Breezes hold their breath.
Sun eclipsed by His act of love.
Submission somber in the air.
Trees tremble in the face of His obedience.
Rocks cry out in protest.
Flowers pale in the presence of such sacrifice.
Deity denied.
Stripped.
Whipped.
Bleeding.
Agony.
Crown of thorns pressed down in mockery.
Spit upon.
Flesh tears.
Abandonment.
Suffocation.
Death.
Silence.
All creation is startled into silence.

Easter Prayer

Sorrow trod with heavy feet
the day that Jesus died.
The rocks cried out, birds did not sing,
the Messiah was denied.

What joyous news, despair is gone!
The news — He did arise!
Hope springs anew, Faith is renewed,
salvation stills men's sighs.

O glorious morn' upon the earth,
the Angels shout for joy.
For wonders worked, God's plan fulfilled
through Mary's little boy.

Oh that we take that Easter morn'
and press it to our heart
with courage, love and faithfulness.
God wills we not depart.

CHRISTMAS

Picture This

The night of "the Birth"
so silently still.
The air of expectation
matching the unnaturally bright stars.
Signaling the coming forth
of the Gift to the World
causes the Universe to stop in awe.
Angels stand motionless in amazement.
Seraphim bow their heads
in acknowledgement of divine Love and Wisdom.
Man plods on in total ignorance
of how the world will change.
Animals stir restlessly,
aware of the excitement in the air.
The Light of the World comes forth
in a golden light of Holiness.
A light rain begins to fall:
Angels' tears of wonder and joy.
The Shepherds standing as allegory
for Jesus, the Good Shepherd, watching over us
as Lambs of God.
Wise men led by the light of a star
foreshadowing Man being led
by the Light of the World.
Mary and Joseph kneel in silent obedience,
knowing that understanding will unfold.
Their total trust and reliance
on the Father now sufficient for them.
The earth trembles in anticipation.

BAH HUMBUG!

Shoppers hunting the Spirit of Christmas
in department stores instead of Church.
Worshiping "things" not Him.
Examining price tags, instead of lives.
Songs of Wonderland, Santas and Snowmen.
Tinkling bells in a world filled
with unheard symphonies.
Praise for displays.
Adulation for the most expensive,
not for the immeasurable Gift of our Lord.
Toys needing everlasting batteries,
superseding the need for Everlasting Life.
Ooohs and Ahhhs at decorated plastic trees.
Unseen is the beauty of our Creator's love for us.
Snowmen and Santas are placed on
the altars of our homes.
Nativity scenes are now the leprous untouchables.
Communion means Christmas parties.
The real magic of the Season
flaking away like fake snow on a fake tree.
Credit a reality and an illusion.
The Spirituality of the season
imploding to a dead beat of the heart.

My God, my God.
Why have we forsaken Thee?

STUNNED INTO SILENCE

Heaven must have been
stunned into silence
when they heard the Father's plan.
That Jesus was to incarnate
and live on earth as man.

Obedience to the Father
from the Holy Parents and Son of Man,
(Mary, Joseph and Jesus)
without question obeying His plan.

Bound in strict obedience
to the Father thro' perfect love.
Jesus lay down His life
so we may live in His love.

Hope

GRANDCHILDREN

A chance to
once more, once again
love.
God's lessons
in Agape* Love
taking form.

Loving
for the sheer joy of loving.

Giving
with no thought of return.
The best of the human spirit
personified for us.

The seasons of our life now arranged
so we have time to spend
saving each sweet morsel
of the moments of life.

A chance to love our children
through them
in a better way.

Grinding our mistakes
with mortar of love
and pestle of wisdom
pouring it out upon
our children's children.

*Agape Love is unconditional love

A Baby

A measure of Grace.

Innocence personified.

Definition now, of Family.

New life inspiring
awe within us.

Knowing that God
smiles upon us.

Created is us, with us
and through us.

Wonder of wonders
sensed in this act of Creation.

The agape* love of God.

Precious, precious Life.

Hope for the future
wrapped in a diaper.

*Agape love is unconditional love.

Seeking The Ruin of Souls

Prowling the World Like a Lion

Keep me in Your shadow, God.
Keep angels in front of me, behind me,
to the right and to the left of me
that I may never turn from you.

As I perceive more and more the face of Evil upon the earth,
I cower and burrow to your side,
hiding in your protection
for I am so afraid.

Evil hides its' face nevermore.
I see it dart from its' hiding place, how bold it is becoming!
Standing arrogantly to languidly survey its' chaos
with careless and indifferent glances.

Pausing amidst the tendrils of smoke
and the last licking flames of destruction.
Looking upon Suffering with contempt
as if of little import, not worthy of attention.

To smile with disdain as it glances around,
eyes darting here and there not wanting to miss,
amidst its' devastation, any chance
to crush any morsel survived.

I sense the waiting, the readiness of the Seraphim,
and Archangels gazing upon the wickedness,
stirring imperceptibly in restlessness.
Stayed by the hand of God, — not yet, not yet.

(Cont'd next page)

(Cont'd *Prowling the World Like a Lion*)

      The outrage,
      the wrath
      of Purity
      as it is offended.

"Vengeance is Mine" saith the Lord
      in a whisper
      that is a shout
heard throughout the Universe.

From the Pits of Hell

Hollow men with withered souls
stride the world causing and ignoring
death, starvation and terror
in the path of their ambitions.
Broken hearts, broken lives.
Extraordinary brutality now ordinary.

An immutable law:
"For every action there is an equal
and opposite reaction"
What price will they pay?
The piper must be paid.

The world stands expectantly, waiting to see
what evil atrocity and obscenity they will next commit.
They seem to come from the pits of Hell.
So where are they going?

Oh, that their evil plans would fall apart
as sand sifting through their fingers.

GIRL CHILD UNHEARD

I am a child without a cry.
Tidily scraped away.
Cleanly vacuumed away.
WHO WILL WEEP FOR ME?

I'm 'inconvenient'.
I'm not 'perfect'.
I'm not 'wanted'.
WHO WILL WEEP FOR ME?

My tiny heart beating
Though they claim I'm not alive.
Tiny eyes forming
Though they'll deny my right to see.
WHO WILL WEEP FOR ME?

Tiny fingers
will never hold my Mother's hand.
Tiny feet
will never run to meet my Dad.
WHO WILL WEEP FOR ME?

If a woman has a right to say
what happens to her body,
WHO WILL SPEAK FOR ME?
For I am woman too!
In Heaven, I will weep for you.

Job 31:14-15, Psalm 139:13-16
Job 1:5, Proverbs 6:16

QUESTIONS

Finally ... Understanding!

God made the flowers,
He also made the rain.
He created love and laughter,
He then allowed us pain.

For if we knew not one,
Would we know the other?
If we knew not loneliness,
Would we care for each other?

If we didn't have sorrow,
Would we be joyful still?
If there were no striving,
Could our hearts be fulfilled?

If there were no tears,
Would laughter fill the air?
If there were no loss,
Would our hearts learn to care?

If we did not yearn
For a glimpse of His face,
Would we ever understand
The meaning of His grace?

ET TU?

It took me a while
to stop treating God
as a foreman and
I was the Boss.
Make so and so do thus and so.
Stop whomever from
doing whatever.

Have you done this too?

It came as a shock
(and embarrassment)
when I realized
what I was doing;
assigning Him problems with MY idea of how
they should be handled.
(Did I think He wouldn't know what to do,
or be able to figure it out?)

Have you done this too?

Now I know that prayer is:
Praise, Petition and Thanksgiving.
Kind of like a conversation with your best friend
who just "happens" to be
King of all Kings
and is Creator of the universe.

Do you do this too?

Who Are You?

Is everyone alone?

Have you found peace
as a companion?

Is your life empty or have you found
Grace along the way?

Is every day cloudy or do you
make your own sunshine?

Do your ears hear gossip
or do you hear the songs of Angels?

Is your life dark or
do the precious gems of children
and friendship light your days?

Have you found meaning in your life
or do you shop to fill that lack?

Have you learned to find the goodness
in people and situations?

Or is bitterness and criticism
the frame around the window of your world?

Were you aware
this was all around you?
Even when you are alone
the room is full

THE CLOCK IS TICKING

Is there enough time
to turn our face
from a neighbor who has need?

Is there enough time
for hatred not to poison others
when you make hearts bleed?

Is there enough time
to not say "I'm sorry"
before you say goodbye?

Is there enough time
to change the consequences
when you tell a lie?

Is there enough time
to give family an abundance of love
so in their hearts you stay?

Is there enough time
to thank and glorify God
even if we unceasingly pray?

Stargazer

What lies beyond that final star?
In blackness, in starlight
the sky has beckoning lights
that seem to signal Joy.

Beyond the darkness
that portends the unknown,
there seems to be more.

We look up as if
we know that's where
all questions and answers lie.

We look with awe, wonder
and yearning, our hearts burning.
No thoughts but open-ness
to infinity, to eternity.

MEN OF GALILEE

(Angels appeared to the Disciples)

"Men of Galilee", they said:

"Why do you stand here looking at the sky?"

Isn't that just a great question?

Couldn't that be asked of Believers today?

Acts 1:11

....

"Go into all the world and preach
the good news to all creation."

Mark 16:15

Busy Doing Nothin'

"I'm not worthy" we protest.
"No kidding!" they reply.
"I'm not holy" I humbly proclaim.
"We understand" they agree with a sigh.

"I never pray for myself" I declare.
And … "Give those jobs to others."
"I can't do any work for the church.
I can "only" pray for our brothers."

Am I not a child of the King?
He's counted the hairs on my head.
I'm so busy being humble
the glory He gives me is dead.

Who is to do the work of God
as we stand and beat our breast?
With all of our self-righteous protests
do we really give Him our best?

When I tiptoe around in the Dark,
how can I walk in the light?
If I hide my light under a bushel
do I praise Him for glory and might?

You probably won't agree with me.
It's purely a point of view —
If I don't start praying for me,
how can I pray for you?

(Cont'd next page)

(Cont'd *Busy Doing Nothin'*)

"They'll Know That We Are Christians
By our Love" we loudly do sing.
Yet I make my faith so unattractive,
is this the real Jesus I bring?

Throw off the mourners weeds I cry.
Let His love and joy be the light.
May I be an example to others;
the dawn dispelling the night.

May I walk with a joyful heart
with smiles and comfort for all.
May I walk in my Saviors love only
so others will feel the call.

Oh, foolish, selfish, narrow view.
Prideful and self-seeking heart.
My pride in being unworthy
takes focus from doing my part.

For if I am unworthy.
So probably are you, my friend.
While everyone's busy doing nothing
Christian living and loving will end.

Yes, I AM unworthy.
Perfection — there is only one.
But, unless we all do something.
Nothing will ever get done!

James 2:17

Who? What?

Who am I
that You would die for me;
Your life burned out
upon that lonely tree.

From Glory came Redemption
to shape our lives so low
that His love,
we each could feel and know.

"What is man that
You are mindful of Him?"

Hebrews 2:6

All?

Why do we make it so little
as we explain why it is we pray?
When crisis knocks on the door
we explain: "All we can do is pray."

We make it sound so useless:
An ineffective thing we do.
'all we can do is pray' indeed!
What a pitiful point of view.

He was present at Creation.
From the Father, He is the Son.
'All we can do' is turn to Him?
It's through His blood we are won.

The power of the Spirit comes
when we pray with love.
"All" we can do is pray to Him?
His glory's my strength from above.

We have no understanding
Of the power of His love.
"All" we can do is pray to Him?
His glory's my strength from above.

"All of you come to the Father
through Me" He came to teach.
Who else would you turn to in trouble?
Whose help should you seek and beseech?

(Cont'd next page)

(Cont'd *All?*)

Do we simply try to be humble
as we bow our heads and say
"Oh my dear, we can do nothing
"All" we can do is pray.

"They'll Know That We Are Christians By Our Love"
we loudly do sing.
Yet I make my faith so unattractive,
is this the real Jesus I bring?

Throw off the mourners weeds I cry.
Let His love and joy be the light.
May I be an examle to others:
the dawn dispelling the night.

May I walk with a joyful heart
with smiles and comfort for all.
May I walk in my Saviours love only
so others will feel the call.

Oh, foolish, selfish, narrow view.
Prideful and self-seeking heart.
My pride in being unworthy
takes focus from doing my part.

For if I am unworthy,
so probably are you, my friend.
And while everyone's doing nothing,
Christian living and loving will end.

Yes, I AM unworthy.
Perfection – there is only one.
But unless we all do something,
nothing will ever get done!

Romans 8: 26-32-37
James 5:16
James 2:17

Everyone, Everywhere

Lost opportunities
when we do congregate,
when we do celebrate
only with those who
believe as we do.

How do we educate,
how well do we elucidate
when we witness only to
those who believe as we do.

How can we witness,
how to show our fitness
as bringers of the Light,
of salvation in the night
for only those who
believe as we do.

How can we contemplate,
how do we formulate
exactly what we receive,
precisely what we believe
sharing only with those who
believe as we do.

How can we be so blind
loving only our own kind?
Wanting our Lord to please,
instead we act like Pharisees.

(Cont'd next page)

(Cont'd *Everyone, Everywhere*)

How do we open eyes,
when do we realize
we're supposed to witness to
those who don't believe as we do.

Though we're not of this world,
we are in this world
and here is where we'll do our work,
here is where we're not to shirk
bringing Jesus to
those who don't know Him as we do.

Preaching to the choir
oh, we ourselves admire
when we tell each other
instead of our lost brother
so they can know Jesus as we do.

How can we appreciate
when we won't elevate
the Word as joy to share
with loving heart and loving care
showing them that they too
can know Him as we do.

How can our faith be strong,
how can we be so wrong
to not want to share
with everyone, everywhere
to know salvation as we do.

Luke 5:30-31

Second Thoughts for When You Have a Minute

Was there a reason
they were called
BEATITUDES
and not ...
DO-ATTITUDES?

....

The Martha Complex

I can get so busy
DOING
I have no time for
BECOMING!

Luke 10:38-42

....

The SUN sets ...
The SON is always shining!

John 8:12

....

"I AM"
is the reason
I am.

Exodus 3:14

(Cont'd *Second Thoughts for When You Have a Minute*)

Faith is a journey.
Life is a journey ...
Pack your baggage carefully.

....

GRANDCHILDREN
are God's equivalent
of having dessert
every day.

....

When I think I understand God,
something, somehow
makes me realize I've made Him
too small.

(5 years later, I read this in my church bulletin)
"It's probably for the best we err in thinking about God most when we imagine we've got God figured out"

....

We don't have to be
PERFECT for God to use us.
We only have to be
WILLING.

(Cont'd *Second Thoughts for When You Have a Minute*)

We have to magnify
the Lord
with prayer and praise
until we grasp
that He is bigger
than our problems.

....

I was
looking at my Bible
and began to wonder,
is your Life bound by
GILT or GUILT?

....

Let my Soul and my Love soar,
oh, my God
so I might come closer to
understanding your Greatness.

Finite can never understand Infinite,
but I would like to be able to
appreciate You more.

....

I think I've finally figured it out
Lord.
The only way to thank you
is through OBEDIENCE.

(Cont'd *SECOND THOUGHTS FOR WHEN YOU HAVE A MINUTE*)

Like Alice, running pell-mell into Wonderland,
Finding, that inside — she's too big for some places
and for others she's too small.
Trying to make sense out of the world
until she learns the Truth which is:
LIFE IS NOT FAIR

The Bible says:
"TRIBULATIONS MAKETH YOU PATIENT."
Haven't there been times
in your life when ...
Tribulations just "madeth" you tired?

When your hands
are clasped in prayer
they are halfway
to lifting up to heaven.
They are halfway there
to opening your arms to others.

WALK IN LOVE.

As we do, we become.
Do God's will
and
He'll take care of the rest.

Philippians 4:9

(Cont'd *Second Thoughts for When You Have a Minute*)

As we serve and
love our neighbor
we are turning
our lives into prayer.

ENCOURAGE
Don't condemn.

LOVE
Don't point a finger and tell others
what they're doing wrong.

Let not
the heart of man
tiptoe away
from the presence
of God.

Pray twice
before you
speak once.
Or
Pray twiceth
before thou
speaketh onceth.

(Sort of a faux King James' version)

(Cont'd *Second Thoughts for When You Have a Minute*)

In the quiet of my
night and day,
my soul does ponder,
my mind does say"

What is man
that you are
mindful of him?"

....

As you act,
so you'll become

....

Oh Lord, my God,
you reside within
where I've been forgiven
and freed from sin.

....

GOD'S WATCHING:

I gave you the tools.
I gave you the rules.
Now go see what you can do.

(And yes, I'm watching!)

(Cont'd *Second Thoughts for When You Have a Minute*)

HMMMMMMMM!
Why aren't we just honest
and pray for longer arms
to pat ourselves on the back
when we do
something wunnnnnnnnnderful?

....

Everything we do and say
should proclaim
the Glory of God.

....

Bless those ahead of us
for they can show us
we still have further to go.

Bless those who are behind us
for they show us
how far we have come
and what God has done for us.

1st verse — Philippians 3:17, 49
2nd verse — Philippians 3:12-14

....

God is Spirit, pure and true.
God is Love.
God created man in His own image.
Doesn't that thought just give your mind Wings?

(Cont'd *Second Thoughts for When You Have a Minute*)

EPIPHANY (finally!)

I know I'm not stupid
And
I don't live in a cave
But
it's really taken me
a long time to realize
that
I'm not in charge of how other people behave!

....

Dear God, you are so far ...
As near as a whisper,
As far as a star.

....

Hate and Resentment
steal pieces of my heart and my soul,
leaving me less of a person
than I was meant to be.

Lightning Source UK Ltd.
Milton Keynes UK
UKOW04f1055220216

268854UK00001B/240/P